B-FLAT CLARINET FINGERING CHART

B-FLAT CLARINET FINGERING CHART

✺

RYAN MIHALY

NEW MICHIGAN PRESS
TUCSON, ARIZONA

NEW MICHIGAN PRESS
DEPT OF ENGLISH, P. O. BOX 210067
UNIVERSITY OF ARIZONA
TUCSON, AZ 85721-0067

<http://newmichiganpress.com>

Orders and queries to <nmp@thediagram.com>.

Copyright © 2022 by Ryan Mihaly.
All rights reserved.

ISBN 978-1-934832-85-1. FIRST PRINTING.

Design by Ander Monson.

Cover collage and final illustration by Jess Bass.
https://www.jessicabass.com/ IG: @partly_spring

CONTENTS

1st Octave   1
[D♯/E♭] [When tilling]   5
[E] [Mud cracks when it dries]   6
[F] [Mother and son, part 1]   7
[F♯/G♭] [Like a cello]   8
[G] [The mirror]   9
[G♯/A♭] [Like a deep well]   10
[A] [Writ into existence]   11
[A♯/B♭] [The Perseus cluster]   12
[B] [As the mountains erode]   13
[C] [Mother and son, part 2]   14
[C♯/D♭] [Greenish rust]   15
[D] [Angela, Vicente, the vagrant]   16

2nd Octave   19
[D♯/E♭] [More a statue than a note]   25
[E] [In sleep]   26
[F] [Divine bodies]   27
[F♯/G♭] [The sick and the dying]   28
[G] [The pheasant]   29
[G♯/A♭] [Sarcasm]   30
[A] [Mother and son, part 3]   31
[A♯/B♭] [They had to establish contact]   32
[B] [Catalog of embarrassments]   33
[C] [A split second]   34
[C♯/D♭] [Raspberries]   35
[D] [How dark?]   36

3rd Octave   39
[D♯/E♭] [House made of D♯]   43
[E] [Seven little knocks]   44
[F] [Amazing grace]   45
[F♯/G♭] [Waiting]   46
[G] [The reed cracks]   47
[G♯/A♭] [The clarinet speaks]   48
[A] [Meursault, Tatiana, the maximizing man]   49
[A♯/B♭] [Handiwork]   50
[B] [A needle]   51
[C] [Glad to be unhappy]   52
[C♯/D♭] [Mother and son, part 4]   53
[D] [The smell]   54

4th Octave   57
[D♯/E♭] [Vision: chaos of birds]   59
[E] [Vision: eyes seek eyes]   60
[F] [Vision: cartwheeling]   61
[F♭/G♭] [Vision: angels under duress]   62
[G] [Vision: peace]   63

Finale   65

Notes   67
Acknowledgments   69

1ST OCTAVE

You have a clarinet at your disposal, a playable ecology of rubber, metal, resin, and wood. A life form: a ligature that comes loose, a reed that warps, responsive keys. Your body wraps around it accordingly. Fingers have trouble finding their place at first, which is unusual, because the instrument is very approachable, a straight line with nothing to hide. The sensation is like submerging your arm in clear water only to find it foreshortened.

Indeed, the clarinet is elemental. Water is essential to its creation and subsistence, like any organism. If you never put your mouth to it, it cracks and turns barren, desert-like. At this point it becomes a fine display piece, something to hang on the wall, a perfectly rigid fixture for a network of cobwebs, a suitable settlement for dust.

If instead you play it, the clarinet speaks, but not merely in music. It complains like a tenant tired of leaks. Or it whispers cryptic suggestions, which, over time, can be decoded intuitively. It has a habit of throwing open doors to long-forgotten rooms and coercing its neglected contents into some sort of "redemptive, musical abstraction," or so it says.

How do you play it? No greater technique can be taught than trust. Agile fingers, a trained tongue, proper embouchure and posture, while important, are nothing without that private agreement the clarinetist makes with the instrument. Not a selling of the soul, per se, or an exchange with the devil at some crossroads (though that need not be out of the question), but the reverse: a *dispersing* of the soul into the clarinet's ecosystem, bits of it mixing with spit and oil from the fingertips, plus breath. A wind to test the malleability of branches, to prove the tree is not a fixed thing but that, in fact, it sways.

But if the soul *is* to be sold, so be it. It usually makes it back to the original owner anyway, slipping easily off the devil's shelf and up through the cracks of the world.

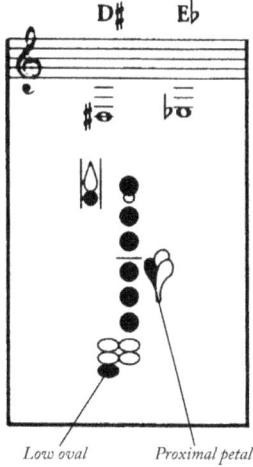

Low oval   *Proximal petal*

[D♯/E♭] When tilling the soil or harvesting fruit, riding a horse or climbing a tree, when praying, both hands and all ten fingers must be used: so it is with D♯, the deepest pitch and the closest to the earth. The integrity of this pitch relies on the strength of the hands' weakest digits: the right little finger, which, holding the low oval, allows the pitch to sound, and the left little finger, which reinforces what the right does by holding the proximal petal along the clarinet's torso. When sounded, the pitch sends shocks to the root canals, granting feral visions; or to the soles of the feet, which feel mud-covered and warm; or to the tailbone, which gives the clarinetist either a sudden bout of vertigo, or the kind of peace only afforded by the eye of a storm.

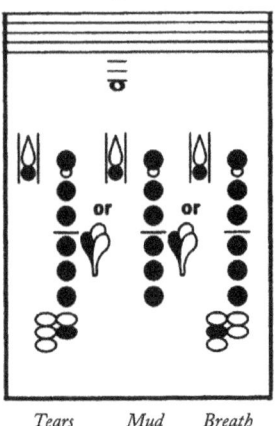

Tears   Mud   Breath

[E] Mud cracks when it dries, texturing the earth. Tears leave streaks when they dry, texturing the face. And breath turns to vapor in the freezing air, texturing it before disappearing. E's three fingerings each evoke one of these transformations. E also gives clairvoyance, though only to very distant times, so distant they are thought to be indecipherable dreams and are often discarded as nonsensical.* A clarinetist wishing to understand these visions should sit barefoot and bare-bottomed in the mud during springtime and plunge all ten fingers—since they are all in use for E—into the wet earth, remove them and let the mud dry until text saturates the hands. Then read the hands.

* See fourth octave.

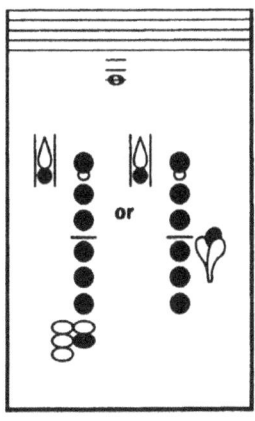

Youth   Verge of death

[F] There is a child sitting in a square basement room. Around him are rows of empty chairs, ordered stacks of blank books and papers, and a window looking out at a small brick courtyard. Through it he can see the grass grow and die. He can see a wall. Every day at noon, someone walks by, barefoot, and the window blazes: this is when the child sings a low F. The paradox of the child with the bass voice is a metaphor for the clarinet. The instrument manipulates the voice so that even a soprano sounds three octaves deeper. Filtered through the clarinet, all voices are equalized and no longer give any indication of age: an F is an F played by a boy or a man on the verge of death. No matter your age, you must envision the chairs filled with loved ones and the child as your son. Then write his name in the blank books and papers. The child and the practiced clarinetist will smile, but you cannot let the smile loosen the tongue's grip on the reed.

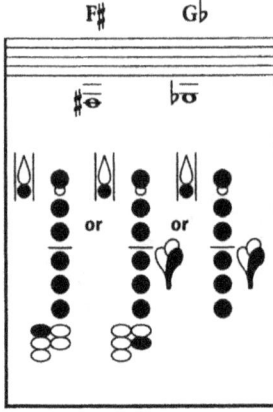

[F♯/G♭] Someone in the room turns your way when you play F♯; they did not expect to hear a cello. They see you playing the clarinet, of course, but they do not see how you are imagining yourself playing it, like a cello, your tongue and breath sending a bow of air sliding through the body of the clarinet. Imitation is the sincerest form of flattery, and in this case there is no other option: the clarinetist who does not imitate the cello makes a dull, hollow sound, like a dying owl—which, in the end, could be the sound you're after. Mimicry is unavoidable and must be cherished, for mimicry is another form of authenticity. A chameleon isn't fake for blending in with a tree.

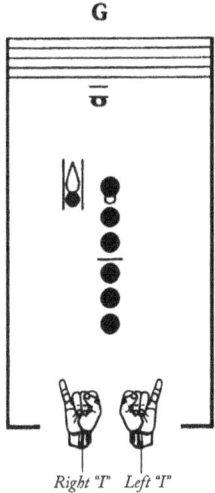

Right "I"   Left "I"

[G] Low G is symmetrical. The little fingers are not in use. However: remove your hands from the clarinet and see you are signing two I's. The two I's are you. A mirror can be used to produce an image of yourself in reverse, a distortion, yet this misleading "I" is satisfactory for confirming the reality of the true "I" you think you are. G is the mirror, reversing everything around it except for itself. A mirror before another mirror creates infinite mirrors; far into this endless repetition is darkness where the imagination runs free. Two clarinetists playing this pitch together produce the same thing, aurally. Other instrumentalists ask to tune to your G: you, clarinetist, are their tonal mirror, to which they adjust their necks, turn pegs, tighten or loosen their lips.

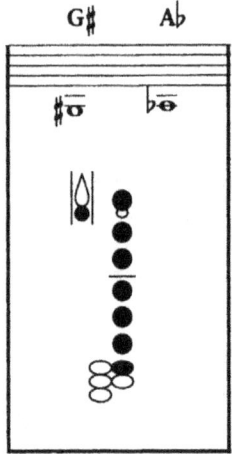

[G♯/A♭] Unstable and agitated, Low G♯ cringes its way through the clarinet's body and out through the bell, disturbed like a swath of earth casting off acres of brick and tar, sickened like a body rejecting a foreign organ. Low A♭, using the exact same fingering, is heavenly-sweet, peaceful, a solitary heron in winter slowly cutting the air to swim in the silver lake, shimmering. The clarinet is like a deep well: some spend their days dropping rocks into it, just to hear the silence of the abyss; others hear their voices gloriously magnified when they sing into it. The difference between G♯ and A♭ depends entirely on the way the clarinetist approaches this darkness.

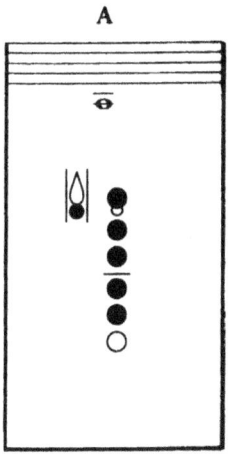

[A] Whether the universe was sung, danced, or writ into existence, whether it started with a bang or a little flick of the wrist, it seems a drawer was flung open on a whim and everything spilled out into perplexing "order." Any list of objects is only a small index of the abundance, but hints at the breadth of the cosmogony: a ceramic mug decorated with flamingos sits atop a newspaper that was just used to crush a mosquito. The tableau takes advantage of your attention, coercing you to mold it into a story. The mind, alight with associations, drawing arrows from object to object, will also devise a numerology for A: 6 keys pressed down, one for each flamingo on the mug, one for each leg of the mosquito… the myth need only persuade the clarinetist, who should use it as a mnemonic. The audience won't hear this, but don't be surprised by the one listener who does.

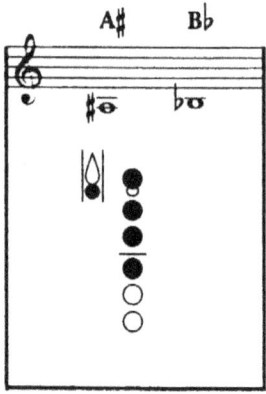

[A♯/B♭] 250 million light years away, a supermassive black hole in the Perseus cluster hums B♭, the same note a jackhammer and a choir hum, the same note a bell clangs to announce a funeral or the arrival of a message on your phone. Then your empty stomach, sensing an entrance, rumbles its request in harmony. Before you eat, walk outside and find noise. Meditate on the long work of glaciers, the slow cleaving of valleys, the formation of the ocean floor, Mesozoic rock colliding and constructing a world. Concentrate on the slow music of centuries. Lodged in the static of the traffic around you is a B♭ stuck like burdock in a garden. Pull at it until it crashes into your chest, leaving a tattoo. The body is the first drum, the first sympathetic string. Music embodied, tonality embroidered into the flesh: now you can eat.

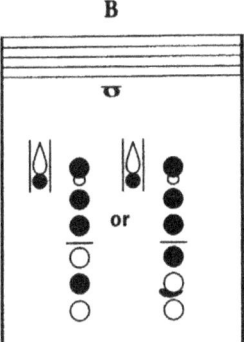

[B] As the mountains erode, tulips grow, teeth loosen from a girl's gums, as arms and legs leave imprints on sheets, so does B seem to hinge on change, suggest difference, turn black or red depending on the season. The right hand is leaving. For the next 13 notes it could be suspended in heaven, or in a pocket, mingling with angels or dust, or in a tree gathering oranges. Occasionally it will mail a postcard back to the left hand to distract it from its task. But for now, for B, the right hand's hold on the clarinet is focused like a spider in the center of its web, steady even as its house bounces in the wind. Practice makes pretense until you slither out of distraction's grasp. Who holds whom? Breathe undivided attention into B. It responds with a swan song, that is to say, the death knell of disruption, which means an afterlife (in this life) of creation.

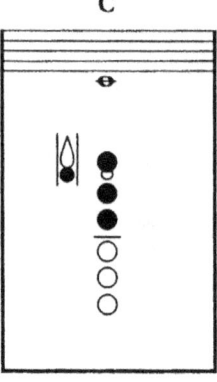

[C] One day at noon, winter sun blazing, your son gets up and raps on the window with his left hand. First, it sings back C; then a woman, barefoot, walks over and peers inside, pressing her right hand to the glass. Your left hand is your son's, holding down the top four keys, knocking on the window, producing the pitch. Your right hand is, for the first time, free. Instead of sending it up trees, spread your fingers, like the woman, over the warmth slowly radiating through the cold pane. C is the sound of recognition: should you see the woman as yourself, the boy's mother, the pitch will sound loved; see them as strangers, and the clarinet will squeak; you will want to put it down for good.

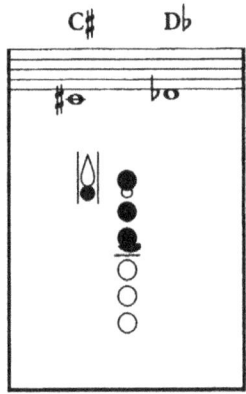

[C♯/D♭] In the narrow alley of the clarinet, regions of greenish rust form with every drop of spit. This inner landscape is open ground for discord: you want C♯ but get a frog instead, a note that gurgles into the air and through the nervous system. This causes terror at the recital. You clear your throat as if the error was there. You adjust your fingers uselessly, for they are already perfect. Finally you think *posture* and straighten your slouch to no avail. There are two ways to breathe but one way to play the note, one way for smoke to leave the chimney, gracefully curling, and C♯ is squealing, wobbling ugly like a top knocked off course. The clarinet's inanimate attitude has more to do with this than you'd like to admit. Sometimes the song that embraces you also impales you. More air will (usually) do.

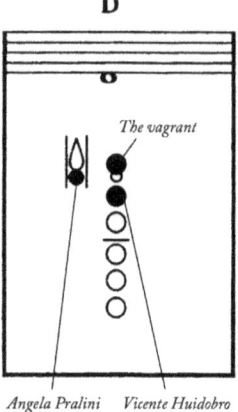

[D] There is a woman named Angela Pralini. She lives on a nondescript street in a novel in Rio de Janeiro and imagines herself a vibrant and crystalline burst of clarinet. She writes a letter to a poet in Chile named Vicente Huidobro, asking him: what will the Last Judgment sound like? She translates his reply: "Guttural violins accompanied by piano and winds thrashing God." She shows these words to the young man who spends his nights sleeping under the awning of a bank, ignored by passersby and police alike, who looks three times his age, who wears a cross around his neck. He sits up from beneath his blanket of newspapers and whispers, "Execration for the dead who do not see…!" and goes back to sleep. This man is your index finger, Angela your thumb, Vicente your middle finger, obscene yet indispensable.

2ND OCTAVE

Some say music is a language. If it is, you should be able to order coffee or declare war with it. If not, then why does it seem to be soliciting me?—you might ask.

Music beseeches and bemoans, or says nothing at all. It is highly impractical. It cannot provide directions or explain itself before a jury.

No one has been subpoenaed or sentenced to death with music.

Russian can be translated into English, but neither can be translated into music. The clarinet uses neither the Cyrillic or Latin alphabets.

Written music is a schematic for the specific movement of body parts along an instrument. Your fingers are dancers in a discotheque called the clarinet.

Language is perfectly capable of describing music, but not the other way around. Instead, music envelops language in colorful robes that help get the point across.

A judge delivering a death sentence wraps his words in the most straightforward music possible in an effort to reduce the chance of misinterpretation.

Advertising stuffs music with sawdust, directing all its beseeching toward a product.

Advertising beseeches and bemoans. But unlike music, it is highly persuasive and straightforward.

Music is often used to set the mood, but moods are temporary, and some songs are longer than a lifetime.

If your family is coming to visit, music would not be enough to tell them it rains every day, that they should bring a coat.

A strawberry is called *ichigo* in Japanese, *truskawka* in Polish, *fresa* in Spanish, but in music?

You can't ask for someone's hand in marriage with music alone, unless a certain melody meant exactly, *will you marry me?*

Music can express joy, sorrow, longing, melancholia, and euphoria without the use of words. But music cannot express hunger, the weather, opinions, grocery lists, dollar amounts, glossaries, rules, or names without the use of language or some sort of subjective or poetic intervention.

You are free to analyze a Bach cantata any way you like, but any interpretation of a stop sign other than "stop" is life threatening.

There is no equivalent of harmony in language except metaphorically. Someone who hears two (or more) words spoken at the same time will probably say, What? Whereas two (or more) notes at the same time are so lovely they get their own names: F major, G# minor, C suspended—to name a few.

A singer who is harmonizing with another singer will often close an ear in order to more accurately produce the pitch. If instead the singers were speaking to each other, the same gesture would be taken as a sign of discomfort, of dissonance.

But why exactly does the singer close an ear? To better hear the inner voice. The same could be said of the writer—poet, speechwriter, dramaturge or propagandist—who might close one ear to the world in order to fine-tune their ideas.

Musical harmony is vertical, instantaneous. Harmony in language occurs over time.

Harmony in language produces miracles like ideas, equations, dissertations, or poetry, all of which are intimate with music, so intimate the borders between them seem to dissolve.

But when poetry gazes into music's eyes and says, "How do I love thee, let me count the ways," music replies with a lyrical crescendo in triple meter originally written for cello but transcribed for clarinet, transposed up an octave and marked rubato.

It's not that music is unreasonable; it simply does not use reason the way language does. Listening to the sound of a flute, one never says, "I agree."

There is no equivalent of rhyme in music except metaphorically. "Love" and "dove" rhyme, but what rhymes with the sound of a clarinet?

Perhaps the oboe and saxophone rhyme with a clarinet, but certainly not a garbage truck or an eagle, you say. But have you heard a clarinet screeching?

If all language were lost except music, what would you say on your deathbed? No last words, just last rhythms, last melodies, painfully beautiful but impossible to decipher—for how would anyone know that you were trying to say you buried your will in a box in the backyard?

Language has more to say about music than music has to say about music.

Music is not concerned with the truth, but language constantly battles with it.

The clarinetist should take note of these responsibilities.

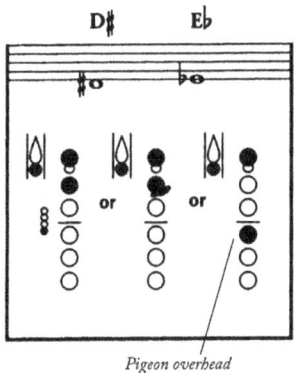

Pigeon overhead

[D♯/E♭] D♯ can't be bothered; it's more a statue than a note, all fixed in marble and glistening in the rain, a meeting point for those who have lost their way, tall and historical and noble; though many find it "ignorable." So the clarinetist should play the irony of this word, the way it calls attention to something not worth calling attention to, and rejoice knowing music has no words to fret with, no preposition to whisk away from the end of the sentence like it's in danger. The only danger here is that one of these fingerings is flatter than the others. Play it and a pigeon shits on the statue's head. Critics and know-it-alls arrive on the scene and cry (they prefer "lament") in a drone not dissimilar to a dying owl.

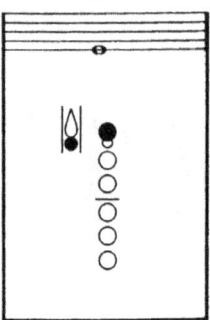

[E] In sleep, your voice leaves the larynx and visits the liver, where your other faculties have gathered to talk about birds. Here your sense of morality asks, "If a cardinal can discern a worm from a blade of grass, can it tell the difference between right and wrong?" to which your memories chuckle and your habits say, "No." Your voice, ever logical, thinks it would be helpful to ask. It mimics the varieties of birdsong as it makes its way up the trachea. Suddenly you're speaking: "Five reasons! Five reasons! Glimmer-glimmer. Five reasons! Glimmer-glimmer." You wake up in a fit of coughing as a magpie swoops by, ignoring you as usual - whereas E waits with bated breath. Why speak, clarinetist, when you can sing? The clarinet can turn your voice into a chickadee's. You fall back asleep and dream of E caught between the top of your lungs and the tip of your tongue, tangled and mute, clarinet disassembled in its box.

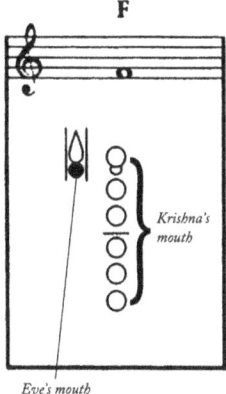

[F] There is nothing to gain from bated breath except atrophied music. F cannot subsist on anything but fullness, so fill your lungs to bursting. There's no mistaking an F that's been supplied with more than ample air: it explodes, it commands, it annoys. Listeners make nasal associations. You are alternately embarrassed and thrilled, like Eve in her sudden nudity. You notice drops of sweat crawling around your neck. You start to smell. Suddenly you want to try something friskier, so you play a song about finding Adam and populating the world. You owe your humanity to apple-eating Eve, the fact that you shut yourself behind a curtain when you shower only to step out later into the presence of a cat, who, gazing at your body with indifference, offers a nostalgic glimpse of Paradise. Krishna, meanwhile, opens his mouth and shows his adopted mother reams of dark energy bursting at the edge of the universe. Eve and Krishna never met—they meet instead at the clarinet. F is the site of the divine in dialogue.

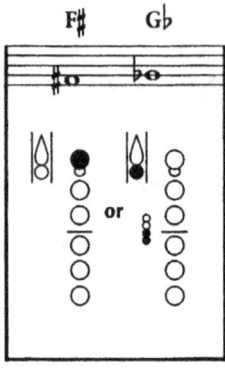

[F♯/G♭] You may need to play for the sick and the dying. The clarinet makes a deathbed a little lighter. Even a healthy body is oriented toward death, but what use is a bone if it's sheltered, never rattles against the hard crust of the earth, if, in other words, it never sings? Risk a wound, a broken bone, for the bitter music of pain and an affinity with suffering. Go hungry, beg for alms. What's a life without scars or a cracked spirit? Ishmael suffered a stormy November of the soul and went sailing; you pick up a clarinet. The day comes when a friend needs a song, that lullaby you know, beginning with a quiet G♭, slow like senescence in autumn, gentle enough to soften the serrated edges of affliction. Music is a reprieve for the miserable. A provision, a ration of God. Breathe misery into your lungs as if the note alone could cure.

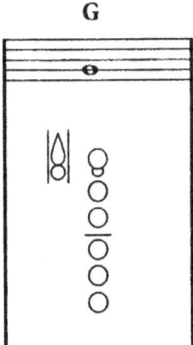

[G] What treasures does a forest hide? Nests of gold, the apparition of a pheasant, a cesspit of flies and worms, bright petals reduced to slime… the forest stretches all the way to the road where a gutter yawns open, inviting a glimpse into an underworld of prowling raccoons. Their world is your world. The difference between "tuition" and "intuition" is lost on them, though; rather they molt and hunt according to their noses, which for the clarinetist is useful only for detecting who licked the instrument last (usually you). G needs no fingers. Suddenly your nose is activated. A bird, bereft of fingers, is held aloft in air by wings. But a pheasant prefers to run. G, then, becomes grounds for flight, but because you are a flightless bird, you put your hands on your hips instead and strut like a pheasant darting out of the forest, twitching its nose and flashing its glossy feathers.

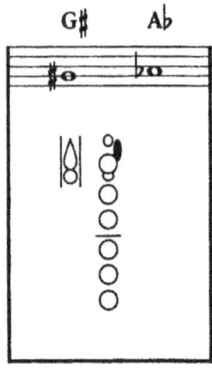

[G♯/A♭] G♯ lives inside the clarinet like sarcasm in a smile, an innocent gesture accidentally tainted with a little twitch of the lip that communicates malice rather than friendship. Worse, certain children read this as a sign of mistrust and deem it an immutable facet of your character. Sarcasm breeds on the face like a sudden disease. It does not take any special adept to extract G♯ as such; you do not need to commit yourself to any order, priesthood, celibacy, or asceticism. In fact it takes little effort at all, one breath at most. Continuing beyond that first breath requires a commitment without any fixed school of thought, though many will make money trying to convince you otherwise. It costs nothing to play. The body is governed in the same way: the veins do not charge the heart for blood.

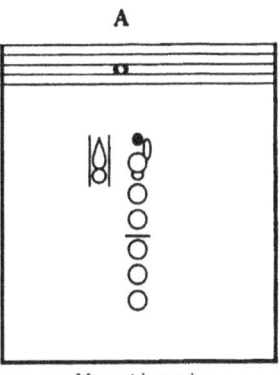

Moon with no cycle

[A] Perfection is a place in the distance. It appears stuck to the horizon. Unlike the woman's smile, growing with the skyline of her city, perfection stays right where it is, fixed, like a moon with no cycle, a permanent blot in the sky. She is crossing the bridge now, and details of the city are starting to appear: the water is gleaming; the train, like a giant unraveling scroll, is carrying messages written in graffiti from one borough to the next; and there, standing on the gray beach on the other side, is her son, gawking at some flock of gulls as always. Birds are kinder to the eye than monolithic, unmoving thing the pious and the obsessive crave. The pious and obsessive clarinetist should note that the journey to perfection is endless and learn to make do with walking. Meantime, her city and her son draw closer.

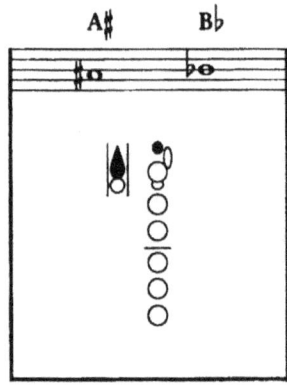

[A♯/B♭] They had to establish contact somehow. Living on opposite sides of the valley, each atop their own mountain, it was clear a bridge would be impossible to build, so it was only appropriate they devise a method of communication. When they met in the valley they agreed on using lights, assigning meaning to darkness at precisely determined intervals. This way, simple communication also became a game with which they could ward off death by shining bright beams in its megalomanic eyes. "Seeing the mundane and witnessing the sublime is less than an eye-blink away," one of them signaled to the other, mimicking a winking eye with her giant spotlight. Their hyena-laughter illuminated the valley that night, disturbing, for a few hours, the mating patterns of the real hyenas with whom they shared those less lonely mountains.

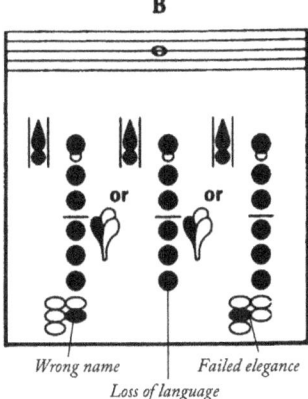

Wrong name   *Failed elegance*
Loss of language

[B] You unwittingly keep a catalog of embarrassments on hand, lifetime-deep, ready to be flipped open to any page should the right moment present itself. The right moment is usually wrong, conventionally speaking: the bus driver doesn't want to hear it, no matter what stop you're at; strangers waiting for the crossing signal don't care; but whenever you happen to remember calling an old friend by the wrong name, or the time you lost all sense of language during an interview, or the failed attempts at elegance, the story comes bursting out. Energy arrives in a constantly unraveling package, ribbons flying everywhere. Often the ribbons get inside the clarinet.

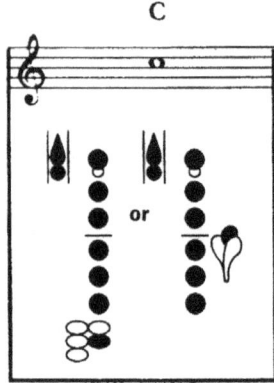

[C] Let us zoom in on a split second. A thread of music in the form of breath passes from your lungs and out toward the bell. Along the way, it passes every closed key like a soul escaping the body, bidding farewell to its first kiss, early terrors, favorite meals, travels, books it read and never finished, its children, their children, and almost gets lost in the enumeration of memories before the air accepts it into its folds, which shifts slightly to make room for this pure but slightly out of tune C. It joins other notes in the air to shape a narrative called melody. Unlike the saints, music leaves no relics behind. There are no fragments of air touched by song enshrined in the churches. Every melody is a martyr, a brief testament of expression that touches the ear and vanishes.

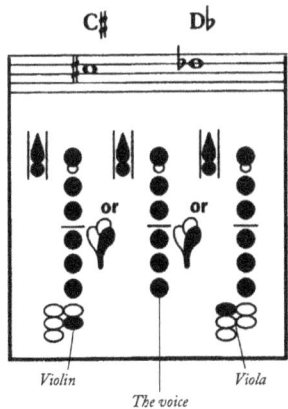

[C♯/D♭] You're not much of a farmer if you spend all day trying to read your raspberries like poems—but it's tempting, considering the patterns they make, the way they taste. So who can blame you, clarinetist, for reading into these charts, your eyes fogged up by black and white circles, seduced by stories you start to see everywhere, stories so layered and numerous it would take the endurance of a dozen Scheherazades to tell them? Will you tell them to your instrument? Rave on like you invented the wheel. Tell the same story from the perspective of the violin, the viola, and the voice—you'll need all night and enough saliva to irrigate a small garden. In the garden a thousand raspberries bloom—but stop in the middle of the story so the sultan will let you live another night.

D

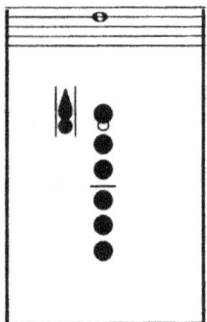

[D] How dark? How dark can you make D? Can you cover it in night? Dress it in black licorice robes? Eliminate any trace of moonlight? Tell the sun not to come back? Each key along the body of the clarinet is a star you must finger, a flame at the end of a wick you must pinch out. Every key an eye you must make blind. Press fists into your closed eyes and follow the patterns that appear. These patterns fill the breath you send down the clarinet with its eyes you hold shut. The patterns dance like snakes inside the pitch, but the pitch is a lake so still it is mistaken for the sky. Practice this until you are synesthetic.

3RD OCTAVE

With your hands wrapped around the clarinet, jaw clenched and tongue tapping on the reed, breath seesawing between your nose and mouth, impressions from the day begin to pool in your mind: the peculiar shape of fog, the fox that crossed you in the street, the red sliver of moon. All the memorable images form an estuary that joins the rivulet of your musical exhalations. By no fault of your own, these waters are stirred by a wind made of nightmares and regrets, misunderstandings and embarrassments, for the music is automatic, each note an amalgamation of everything on the top of your mind plus everything you intend to leave out.

The patterning of your fingers when playing a melody is a translation of this composite psychic mass. The clarinet digests and releases it, creating a disturbance of which music is the byproduct. An audience, if present, is reminded of their childhood, a bird, an excursion, a tragedy.

Or they hear the dancelike quality of the music and began to waltz. Dance is the aftereffect, the instant lineage of music.

Or, embarrassed, they fold their arms and look away. Unwanted music has a way of making you feel naked.

Or they regain clarity that dementia robbed from them.

Or they smile a very private smile. The mathematics of their nostalgia occurs at Mach 1.

Meanwhile, the clarinet starts lecturing you, ranting obscurely like it's fully tenured: "Wait to play G♯! It belongs in one place and one place only. But don't be mistaken, it's not shaped like a shoe, which is obviously for the foot, or a chair for sitting—the moment will come and you will know what I mean. There is little room for error, but the more you tinker with this room, the more innovative you are. For that is where the imagination likes to haunt, that 'little room' way out in the margins. The imagination doesn't *live* or *sleep* there, it just wants to visit as often as possible, so stretch it, shine a light in that little room, show it for what it really is. Some people will enjoy this. Others will call you a sham or a murderer. You will learn to endure these accusations throughout your life, for if you play with any regularity you can be certain they will be hurled at you twice as regularly. Just be certain to clean me every once in awhile, and by the way, do you remember that time as a kid you stole a book…"

This private monologue continues unabated for the length of a concert. The message changes with the weather, with the architecture of the concert hall. One day it's:

"*Hold, mouth, tongue, finger*—place these words before you and neutralize them. Reach into them and pull out what is excessive, ornamental, and sexual. There is no need for an erotics of the clarinet, or a hermeneutics, or any theory other than that of the imagination, that ever-churning force that molds (makes new) and molds (makes old) and molds and molds and molds."

The next it's: "Don't be dispassionate."

As long as you hold a clarinet, you have a front row seat to this rambling sermon.

"To play the clarinet, play the cello. Be polyamorous. Avoid the clarinet, walk around the lake, transcribe the cuckoo cry. The music you need is in the shapes snow and salt make. The sun is music. Mud is music."

"Singing and drumming came first."

"Silence has the right to remain."

The clarinetist should take note of these responsibilities.

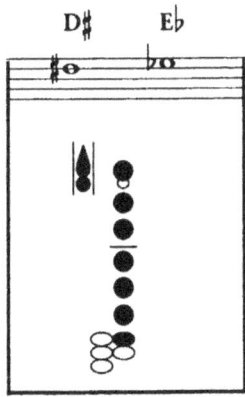

[D♯/E♭] The walls creak and tremble in a house made of D♯. Climbing interminable staircases, turning corners and walking over shrieking floorboards, you listen to rooms that other visitors deem silent and haunted. They *are* haunted—dead wood cut into parallel lines, laid in a grid, and painted white longs for the forest—but they are not silent: your ears are tuned to miniature sounds stirred up by the foot, not those common squeaks but the banshee howls in the upper frequencies that carry on for long minutes after all movement has stopped, when all anyone else hears is silence. The clarinetist will make these sounds, too, with strict training for asymmetric fingerings and a tight embouchure, or a complete lack of experience, as the first attempts at sound are always met with a homesick scream from the reed.

E

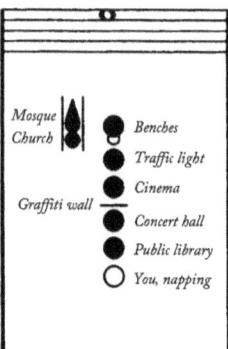

[E] Now there are seven little knocks on the door. Turns out the city wants in, thinks it would be nice to install some benches in the kitchen, set up a designated graffiti wall in the hallway, convert the basement into a public library (you didn't get the message because you nap in the afternoon), build a mosque in the closet, a church in the sunroom, a cinema in either the bathroom or the guest room (there's a dispute), it all seems a bit unmanaged, but who are you to say no? So you say yes, there's plenty of room anyway, you could hang some traffic lights on the stairwell, hire an architect to do the garden… maybe those knocks are just the sound of your fingers getting in place for E, you think… but suddenly you have the keys to the city, so in the end maybe it's best you step up to the podium in the concert hall-turned-garage and make up an anthem before you give this bustling indoor metropolis a name.

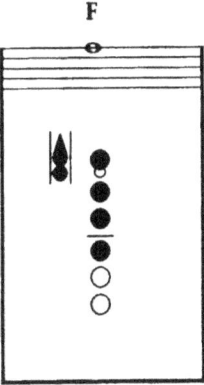

[F] There is a man whose head is in the clouds, clouds so gray and pervasive it's doubtful a sun is shining behind them. Every day he walks the same route around town looking like he's just learned a lesson, one he should have learned much earlier. Sometimes at dusk he sprawls out on a bench by the harbor and screaks at the ocean: "Amazing grace, how sweet the sound, I once was lost, and still I'm lost, was blind and nothing's changed." If he knew he was singing in the key of F, he would undoubtedly call it the Key of Formaldehyde, or the Key of the Forgotten, and though it is not your duty to inform him of such, he still could use a little accompaniment (let alone some company). Play along to his low song until a kid walks by and drops a coin in his hat.

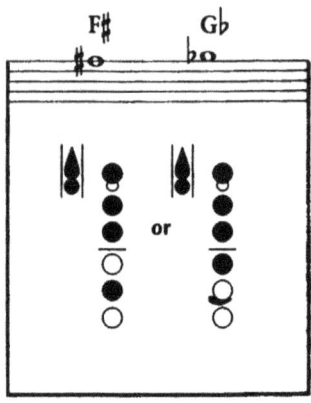

[F♯/G♭] Waiting is a form of absolution, a fasting of action. Time moves around you as you sit there, freeing you from long-forgotten guilt suddenly resurfacing: all the old words and those small, wretched acts flare up once more and disappear for good like a will-o-the-wisp. Then God, that ardent photographer of the soul, appears. He takes a snapshot of your spirit in a state of grace and promises to show it to you the next time you lose track of the truth, that divine virtue that always dissolves into a fog of subjectivity when you consider the myriad reasons behind any action, speechless. The antidote to speechlessness is the consultation of song, such as the bronze hum of F♯ or the low indigo cloud of G♭, and their attendant nostalgias.

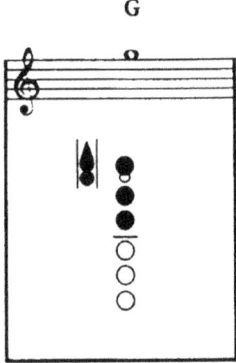

[G] G warrants a walk around town, where you pass a fox pressed into the road, deer eating weeds, a muddled conversation (seemingly jocular) among construction workers, and other ordinary flights of fancy, like children inventing games in the grass and peculiar graffiti, sun blaring over all of it, covering your vision with a screen of radiant green. You rub your eyes to try and get a better picture, but your eyes sink deeper into your head. You wake up sweating. You lick the moisture on your lip and take it to the reed. You've never seen a dead fox before. Thinking this, the clarinet does not respond, so you play harder to compensate. The reed cracks and you swallow its splinters.

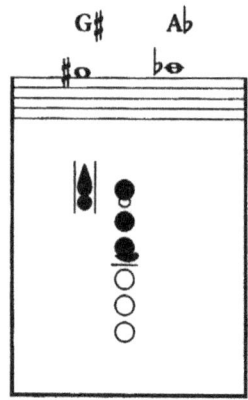

[G♯/A♭] Then the clarinet speaks: "The throat is the reed you must wet. There are splinters in your stomach now. You are hungry. You are hungry and I feed you water. The pit in your stomach deepens. The splinters shift around. You need something to chew to make the teeth work, to gnash or clench, not make them shine like porcelain. I feed you milk and your teeth glisten and the pit only deepens. Listen: a human being is only a reed, the weakest in nature, but he is a thinking reed. To crush him, the whole universe does not have to arm itself. A mist, a splinter, a drop of water, is enough to kill him. But if the universe were to crush the reed, the man would be nobler than his killer, since he knows that he is dying, and that the universe has the advantage over him. The universe knows nothing about this. The throat is the reed you must wet. I am a voice box you hold."

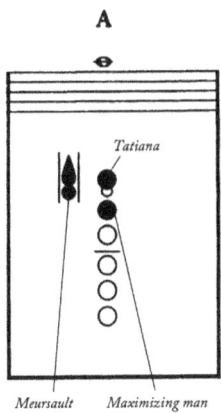

[A] There is a man in a novel named Meursault who spits on the chaplain when he visits him in prison, hours before his execution. He is not much of a believer, and who can blame him. He doesn't know that the cells on either side of him are occupied: to his left is a woman named Tatiana working on her translation of *Don Juan* into Russian from memory. She has just given some of her tiny manuscript pages to a guard who has promised to type them. In the cell to his right is a wrongly accused man praying to all gods at once, "maximizing" (his word) on Pascal's wager. Protesters gather outside for the last time. Your thumb covers Meursault and his spit. Your middle is the maximizing man. Your index must accommodate over a thousand lines of rhymed verse in Russian.

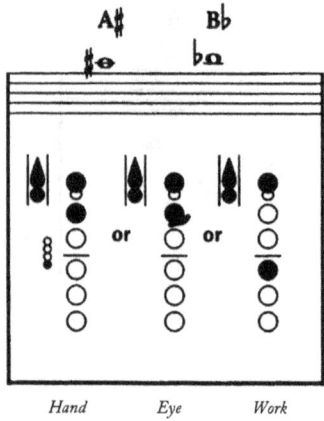

[A♯/B♭] Words are flirtatious and uncertain: one moment they turn you on, the next they turn on you, attaching themselves to your memories and the landscape of everyday life in an endless exchange of betrayal and arousal. Sometimes it seems Babel never fell: all languages are unified in your mind; communication requires only a near-mastery of dialects and vernacular. At other times, seven-syllable words accumulate in your throat forming some inextricable melon-shaped blockage. Meanwhile, birds and children sing outside. Music is not a language because it cannot be translated into anything. It can only be described. A♯, then, is the word "handiwork" mispronounced "hand-eye-work."

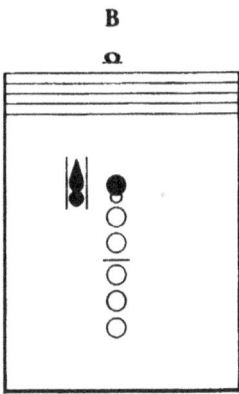

[B] Ease into B the way a needle would into skin. To use your tongue as a needle you need to change the way you feel the tongue. Chew the seeds of a hot pepper. The seeds turn your tongue into a surface that water burns. Swish water around the tongue and swallow. As your tongue sizzles, speak under your breath. Speak so softly you appear to be mouthing promises to God. Now breath is a surface, too, under which you mutter your words, under which the fragility of B is revealed. It may be fragile, but that does not mean it can't be loud. If not a needle, think the other way around: blood seeping out of cracked skin, passing slowly from the veins up to the surface, coloring the hand in lurid reds.

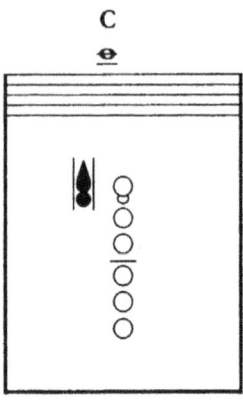

[C] There's a man sitting outside, staring off somewhere, absentmindedly dipping sweets into his coffee. He says: "Blood is to the body as silence is to the soul. I sat for hours and the silence made an impression on my old skin and the hours became years. I learned I'm so glad to be unhappy. So often I've felt like a husk. Nothing more than a doll filled with hot air and grass. Now I see belladonnas and bluebells everywhere, even in the sides of buildings. And magpies, but that's the only bird whose name I know. And bees. I am in love with the pollinators! How they fill the flowers with gold. To enter flowers fully give your life away." Then he whistles a glassy C before he continues his story.

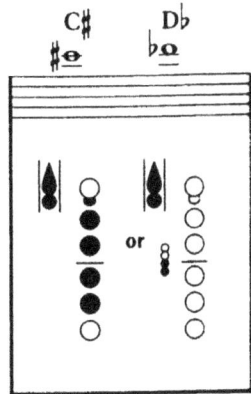

[C♯/D♭] He continues: "My mom's been gone a long time, but I smell her everywhere. I remember it seemed every other Sunday she was spilling some new bottle of perfume, we were always in a rush to church, me running to the bathroom and scooping some up for myself, rubbing it on my neck, once my ribs, once even tasting it. I'd go sit inside by the window when we got home and she'd go right to the garden, hold each flower bulb in her hand one by one, still in her Sunday clothes, and I'd be lost looking at some hummingbird—I know that bird too!—until she'd come over and tap on the window. Tap on it fast with her fingernails, sounded like this." He clinks his coffee cup, C♯—and immediately orders a refill. "Should be a C with a full cup."

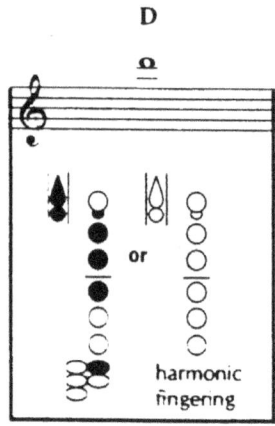

[D] The smell is incredible, new: orange peels and coffee grounds, a noxious mingling of metallic scrap and plastic, anise, oil-smeared foil. Instead of gagging on these fumes they move you, if only for a moment—then the body contorts as it should. But if kept under control, transcendence is here in this monstrous scent that seems to bore into your shuddering skin. So often you look for God with your flashlight on in the middle of the day when he is right under your nose—"she," someone says—and as theologians and feminists start to twitch, you salivate like a beast and pucker up for D which, in the face of theoretical gridlock, is a salve.

4TH OCTAVE

Memory has a way of assaulting your consciousness.
A faint glimmer on water.
Slow peeling of an apple, skin in curls.
Someone, only you know who.
A vision disrupting the order,
a comet,
only uglier.

The clarinet has an antidote to this.
You may think when you play.
Whatever you think it keeps secret.
Not like blood seeping into fabric, better.
Like in one ear and out the other,
mutated to sound.
A slanted language scratched in air
no one understands
the same way.

Who knows if all art
aspires to the condition of music
if music confounds and confuses.

But it makes a fine shield.

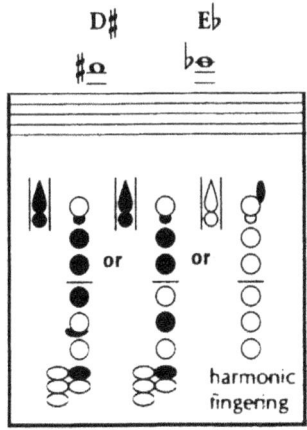

[D♯/E♭] Vision: sun and rain, specks of blue, river flooding over; bare trees, chaos of birds, mad chirping a dramatization of the afternoon, red, wet, widening of the hour—cries, calling, clambering, rain, sun at the top of its arc, invisible cue: chirping sucked back into the collective throat—silence, then buzzing stillness, dripping stasis, distant ice cracking, despite a lack of it nearby; dilating sun, river making mud, wings ruffling, faint chirping again; rain suddenly stopping, daylight looking like someone who has just finished crying, identity torn away, face replaced by revelation.

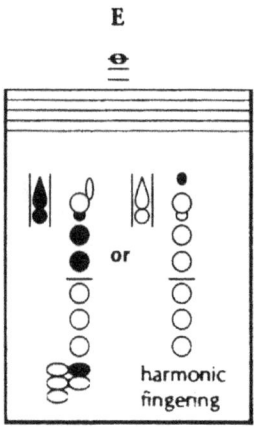

[E] Vision: a bed, night; main roads closed; snow; moon full and haloed—soft glow of faces; words eagerly spilling out of mouths; memory lodged in a wall; silence of space through which eyes seek eyes; fingers enmeshed in space between fingers—hair loosened into heart; hair curling into and out of colors—footfall—flinch; blinked tears; cold wind; color of sky curling hair into footfall—silences growing; silver thread; free, fine weave—laugh-flash of teeth; gleaming skin; children laughing—bite? silence; kiss? rabbit rushing into brush; blameless God watching listlessly, wanting to intervene more directly; moon suddenly making midday appearance.

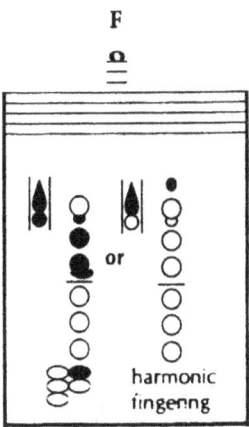

[F] Vision: midday, snow falling, winter sun blazing; blue shadows on bricks lovingly arranged, textured by salt and dirt and footprints, barefoot children cartwheeling and leaping over them because of the game; snow melting making reflecting surfaces, children staring into river-mirrors suddenly forming, seeing self in watery splotches, asking "who?," earth rejecting bricks, bricks flying, children cartwheeling in the mud underneath, hopscotching, counting *one two fee fou*, children asking "who?," someone answering "I, who fell from the sky to lay a mirror on the ground for you," snow falling, snow falling.

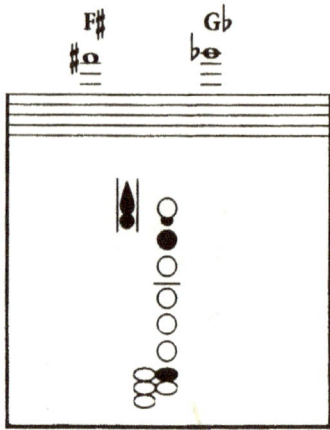

[F♯/G♭] Vision: nighttime foaming at the mouth with stars; angels under duress, roaming the erotic waters of adolescence, enchanted by gossip; revelry in the forest, searching for kinship; rumor mill, speculation, threads lining their clarity net, through which hearsay passes and truth is caught, intensified by darkness and the party; fountain of atmospheres, eruption of hills, reminiscence of an origin, reliving a creation myth; stories realized by a commanding breath; a visit to the beach, shell shrapnel at the ankles, primeval ocean heaving away; primeval pink clambering over the horizon like a timid visitor; everyone wading into daylight to wonder.

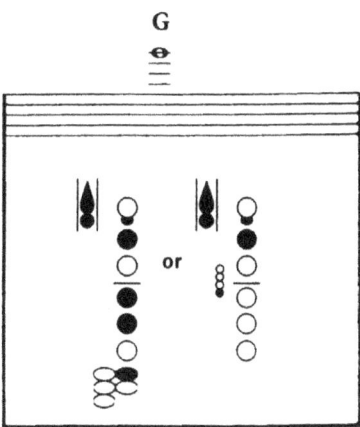

[G] Vision: Peace upon arrival into waking—peace hits the heart—peace metastasizes, peace kills—peace writes its codex on flesh—peace freshens the shelves—peace repeats its plaintive call—you grow bored, peace dies, peace reborn as waning moon, warming water, amniotic déjà vu—as ashes, pine, snowflake aflame, ditto rain—fossilizing peace for who to find, among phrasing of rocks, burning basalt, ever-churning earth, or up, astringent stars curdling sky, multiplying-dying, haggling with eyes for the remainder of nights, remainder being *fou fee two* nights, soon *one,* world eye closing or opening depending on what flags unfurl at the command to play.

The clarinet is a way of seeing.

Which of the billion breaths in your lifetime will you give this humble woodwind?

The first breath is a hiccup, awkward kick-start to a life song.

The final gasp on your deathbed may be all the air you need to keep playing in the pale green light of the afterlife.

In between, music comes in fits and starts.

Of course, the clarinet has a mantra for this:

Mortal to the end
a rule to which we're bound.
Death a dearth of life,
breath the birth of sound.

NOTES

"[D] [Angela, Vicente, the vagrant]"—For more on Angela Pralini, see Clarice Lispector, *A Breath of Life*, translated by Johnny Lorenz. "A vivid and crystalline burst of clarinet" are their words. For more on Vicente Huidobro, please see his book *Altazor*, translated by Eliot Weinberger. "Guttural violins accompanied by piano and winds thrashing God" is an adaptation of their words. For more on the vagrant, see Pablo Neruda, "Nocturnal Statutes" from *Residence on Earth*, translated by Donald D. Walsh. "Execration for the dead who do not see" is an adaptation of their words.

"[A♯/B♭] [They had to establish contact]"—"Seeing the mundane and witnessing the sublime is less than an eye-blink away" is from *The Zen Teaching of Bodhidharma*, translated by Red Pine.

"[F] [Amazing grace]"—I am indebted to James Tate for the word "screaks."

"[G♯/A♭] [The clarinet speaks]"—The section beginning "a human being is only a reed" is an adaptation from Blaise Pascal's *Pensées*, translated by Honor Levi.

"[A] [Meursault, Tatiana, the maximizing man]"—For more on Meursault, please see Albert Camus, *The Stranger*, translated by

Matthew Ward. For more on Tatiana Gnedich, who translated all of *Don Juan* into Russian from memory in prison, please see Efim Etkind's essay "The Translator," translated by Jane Bugaeva.

ACKNOWLEDGMENTS

This book is dedicated to my parents, who got me a saxophone, and to Gabe, who let me borrow the clarinet.

B-Flat Clarinet Fingering Chart first came to life in J'Lyn Chapman's workshops at Naropa—thank you to her, and to the poets in those workshops who were the first readers.

Three artist residencies provided the space and inspiration to finish this book. They are: Greywood Arts in Killeagh, Ireland; Brashnar Creative Project in Skopje, North Macedonia; and Bridge Guard in Štúrovo, Slovakia. My deep gratitude to Jess, Hughie, Ankica, Karol, Hanneke, Gyuri, and Zsofi who run these wonderful places.

Thanks also to Mark Thomas at St. Thomas Aquinas Catholic Center in Boulder for letting me play clarinet in church.

Many thanks to Jess Bass and Wheeler Light for making the cover of this book sing, and to Ander Monson for bringing this bound book into the world.

Poems from this book originally appeared in *Firmament, Tupelo Quarterly, Peripheries, Cutbank Online, Massachusetts Review, Posit, Opossum*, and *DIAGRAM*. Thank you, editors and readers!

Finally, my love & thanks to Karolina, who both came up with the phrase, and is my clarity net.

RYAN MIHALY is is a writer and musician from New England. He graduated from the MFA program at Naropa University where he was an Anne Waldman fellow. His poems, translations, and interviews have appeared in *The Massachusetts Review, Cordite Poetry Review, Asymptote, ANMLY*, and elsewhere. He works at a non-profit music school, teaches saxophones to students of all ages, and is translating (with Karolina Zapal) the work of Polish poet Halina Poświatowska.

❋

COLOPHON

Text is set in a digital version of Jenson, designed by Robert Slimbach in 1996, and based on the work of punchcutter, printer, and publisher Nicolas Jenson. The titles here are in Futura.

❂

NEW MICHIGAN PRESS, based in Tucson, Arizona, prints poetry and prose chapbooks, especially work that transcends traditional genre. Together with DIAGRAM, NMP sponsors a yearly chapbook competition.

DIAGRAM, a journal of text, art, and schematic, is published bimonthly at THEDIAGRAM.COM. Periodic print anthologies are available from the New Michigan Press at NEWMICHIGANPRESS.COM.

www.ingramcontent.com/pod-product-compliance
Lightning Source LLC
Chambersburg PA
CBHW031457040426
42444CB00007B/1130